Watching the Wind

By Edana Eckart

Children's Press®
A Division of Scholastic Inc.
New York / Toronto / London / Auckland / Sydney
Mexico City / New Delhi / Hong Kong
Danbury, Connecticut

Photo Credits: Cover © Peter Gridley/Getty Images; p. 5 © Roger Ellis/Getty Images;
pp. 7, 17, 21 (bottom left) © Photodisc/Getty Images; pp. 9, 11, 21 (top left and right)
© Corbis; p. 13 © James A. Sugar/Corbis; p. 15 © Jim Cummins/Getty Images; pp. 19, 21
(bottom right) © GoodShoot/Superstock
Contributing Editors: Shira Laskin and Jennifer Silate
Book Design: Michelle Innes

Library of Congress Cataloging-in-Publication Data

Eckart, Edana.
    Watching the wind / by Edana Eckart.
    p. cm.—(Watching nature)
    Summary: Simple text introduces facts about the wind.
    ISBN 0-516-27599-2 (lib. bdg.)—ISBN 0-516-25941-5 (pbk.)
    1. Winds—Juvenile literature. [1. Winds.] I. Title. II. Series.

    QC931.4.E25 2004
    551.51'8—dc22

                                                            2003012006

Contents

It is windy today.

The wind moves many things.

5

The wind moves the leaves on trees.

The wind can move the **branches** on trees, too.

During **storms**, winds can be very strong.

9

Hurricanes are storms with very **powerful** winds.

During hurricanes, the winds can even move cars!

People can study the wind.

They use **weather vanes** to learn which direction the wind blows.

13

People use the blowing wind to fly kites.

15

People use the wind to move **sailboats**, too.

When it is very windy, sailboats move fast.

People also use the wind
to do work.

Windmills use the wind
to move water.

The wind can be very powerful.

New Words

branches (**branch**-uhz) parts of a tree or bush
that grow out from the trunk

hurricanes (**hur**-uh-kanez) very big storms over
the ocean

powerful (**pou**-uhr-fuhl) having the ability to do
things or make things happen

sailboats (**sayl**-bohts) kinds of boats that have
one or more sails, or pieces of cloth that catch
the wind

storms (**stormz**) heavy rain, snow, sleet, or hail
with a lot of wind

weather vanes (**weth**-uhr **vaynz**) tools that are
used to find which direction the wind blows

windmills (**wind**-milz) machines operated by wind
power that are used to grind grain into flour,
pump water, or generate electricity

To Find Out More

Books
Can You See the Wind?
by Allan Fowler
Grolier Publishing Co., Inc.

What Makes the Wind?
by Laurence Santrey
Troll Communications L.L.C.

Web Site
Wind Energy
http://www.eia.doe.gov/kids/renewable/wind.html
Learn the answers to many questions about wind
on this Web site.

Index

About the Author
Edana Eckart has written several children's books. She enjoys bike riding with her family.

Reading Consultants

Kris Flynn, Coordinator, Small School District Literacy, The San Diego County Office of Education

Shelly Forys, Certified Reading Recovery Specialist, W.J. Zahnow Elementary School, Waterloo, IL

Paulette Mansell, Certified Reading Recovery Specialist, and Early Literacy Consultant, TX